The World's Continents

AFRICA

Polly Goodman

HODDER
Wayland

an imprint of Hodder Children's Books

The World's Continents series includes:

Cover and title page images: These are satellite photographs taken from space that have been specially coloured on a computer.

Contents page: This satellite photograph shows the clouds swirling above Earth.

Africa is a simplified and updated version of the title *Africa* in Wayland's *Continents* series.

Text copyright © 2000 Hodder Wayland
Volume copyright © 2000 Hodder Wayland

First published in Great Britain in 1996 by Wayland Publishers Ltd. This simplified and updated edition published in 2000 by Hodder Wayland, an imprint of Hodder Children's Books.

A Catalogue record for this book is available from the British Library.

ISBN 0 7502 2868 7

Printed and bound in Italy by G. Canale & C. S.p.A.

Hodder Children's Books
A division of Hodder Headline plc
338 Euston Road, London NW1 3BH

Statistics
Population figures, life expectancy and infant mortality figures in this book are for 1998.
Literacy rates are for 1995.
GNP figures are for 1997.

Sources
United Nations Development Programme
Unicef: *The State of the World's Children, 2000*

Picture credits
Britstock 13; Camera Press 42; Hutchinson 15, 19, 36, 37, 37, 39; Impact 26, 43; Panos 22, 25, 31, 32, 33; Spectrum Colour Library 17; Trip 12, 14, 17, 23, 27, 38–39, 41; Frank Spooner Pictures 11, 23, 27, 29; Wayland Picture Library 19, 20, 24, 26, 28, 29, 34, 35, 40; Zefa, contents page, 10

Map artwork by Peter Bull. Graph artwork by Mark Whitchurch. Globe artwork by Tim Mayer.

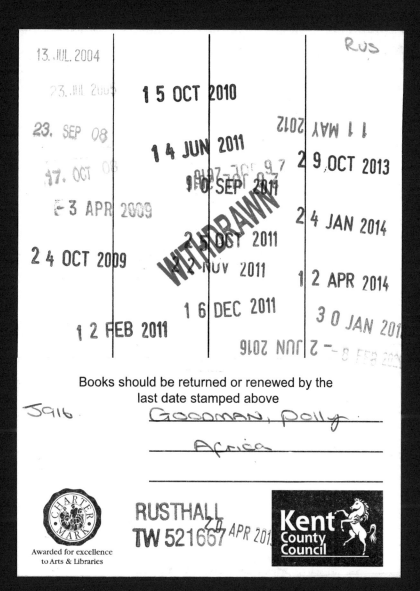

Books should be returned or renewed by the
last date stamped above

CONTENTS

COUNTRIES OF AFRICA

MOROCCO

Area: 446,550 km²
Population: 27,377,000
Main language: Arabic

The maps on the following pages ▶ show the countries of Africa and their capital cities.

WESTERN SAHARA

Area: 266,000 km²
Population: 275,000
Main language: Arabic

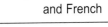

MAURITANIA

Area: 1,025,520 km²
Population: 2,529,000
Main languages: Arabic and French

CAPE VERDE

Area: 4,033 km²
Population: 408,000
Main language: Portuguese

SENEGAL

Area: 196,192 km²
Population: 9,003,000
Main language: French

THE GAMBIA

Area: 10,689 km²
Population: 1,229,000
Main language: English

MALI

Area: 1,248,574 km²
Population: 10,694,000
Main language: French

GUINEA-BISSAU

Area: 36,125 km²
Population: 1,161,000
Main language: Portuguese

IVORY COAST (CÔTE D'IVOIRE)

Area: 322,500 km²
Population: 14,292,000
Main language: French

BURKINA FASO

Area: 274,220 km²
Population: 11,305,000
Main language: French

GUINEA

Area: 245,857 km²
Population: 7,337,000
Main language: French

LIBERIA

Area: 112,600 km²
Population: 2,666,000
Main language: English

GHANA

Area: 238,533 km²
Population: 19,162,000
Main language: English

SIERRA LEONE

Area: 72,325 km²
Population: 4,568,000
Main language: English

NORTH AFRICA

Rabat

MOROCCO

El-Aaiún

WESTERN SAHARA

0 200 400 600 800 km
0 100 200 300 400 500 miles

MAURITANIA

Nouakchott

CAPE VERDE

Praia

Dakar

SENEGAL

Banjul

THE GAMBIA

MALI

Bamako

BURKINA FASO

Ouagadougou

GUINEA BISSAU

Bissau

GUINEA

Conakry

SIERRA LEONE

Freetown

IVORY COAST

GHANA

TOGO

LIBERIA

Monrovia

Abidjan

Accra

WEST AFRICA

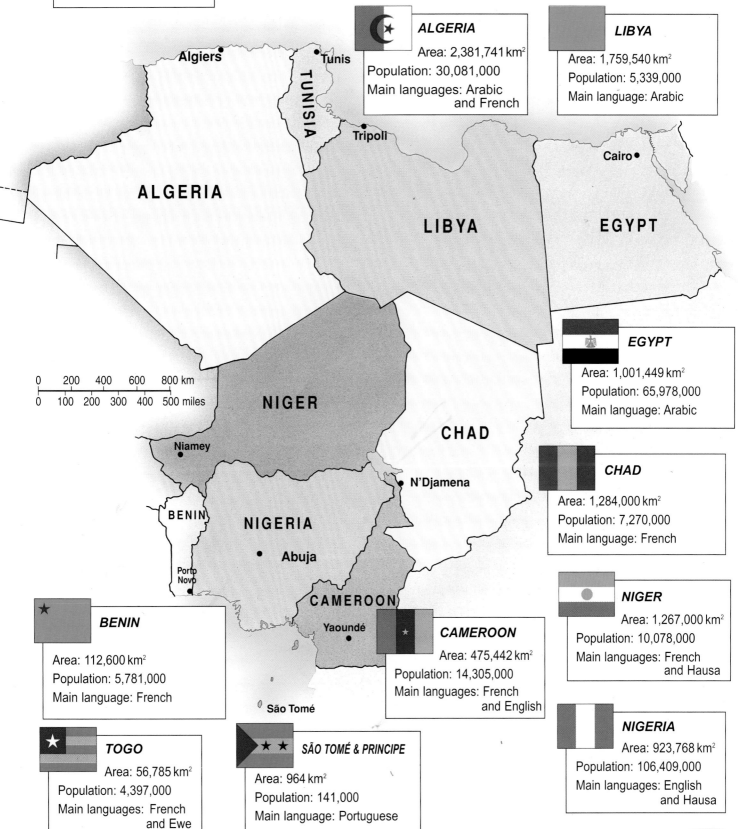

TUNISIA
Area: 163,610 km²
Population: 9,335,000
Main languages: Arabic and French

ALGERIA
Area: 2,381,741 km²
Population: 30,081,000
Main languages: Arabic and French

LIBYA
Area: 1,759,540 km²
Population: 5,339,000
Main language: Arabic

EGYPT
Area: 1,001,449 km²
Population: 65,978,000
Main language: Arabic

CHAD
Area: 1,284,000 km²
Population: 7,270,000
Main language: French

NIGER
Area: 1,267,000 km²
Population: 10,078,000
Main languages: French and Hausa

NIGERIA
Area: 923,768 km²
Population: 106,409,000
Main languages: English and Hausa

CAMEROON
Area: 475,442 km²
Population: 14,305,000
Main languages: French and English

BENIN
Area: 112,600 km²
Population: 5,781,000
Main language: French

TOGO
Area: 56,785 km²
Population: 4,397,000
Main languages: French and Ewe

SÃO TOMÉ & PRINCIPE
Area: 964 km²
Population: 141,000
Main language: Portuguese

Algiers • Tunis •
TUNISIA
Tripoli •
Cairo •
ALGERIA
LIBYA
EGYPT
NIGER
CHAD
Niamey •
N'Djamena •
BENIN
NIGERIA
Abuja •
Porto Novo •
CAMEROON
Yaoundé •
São Tomé

0 200 400 600 800 km
0 100 200 300 400 500 miles

5

CENTRAL AFRICA

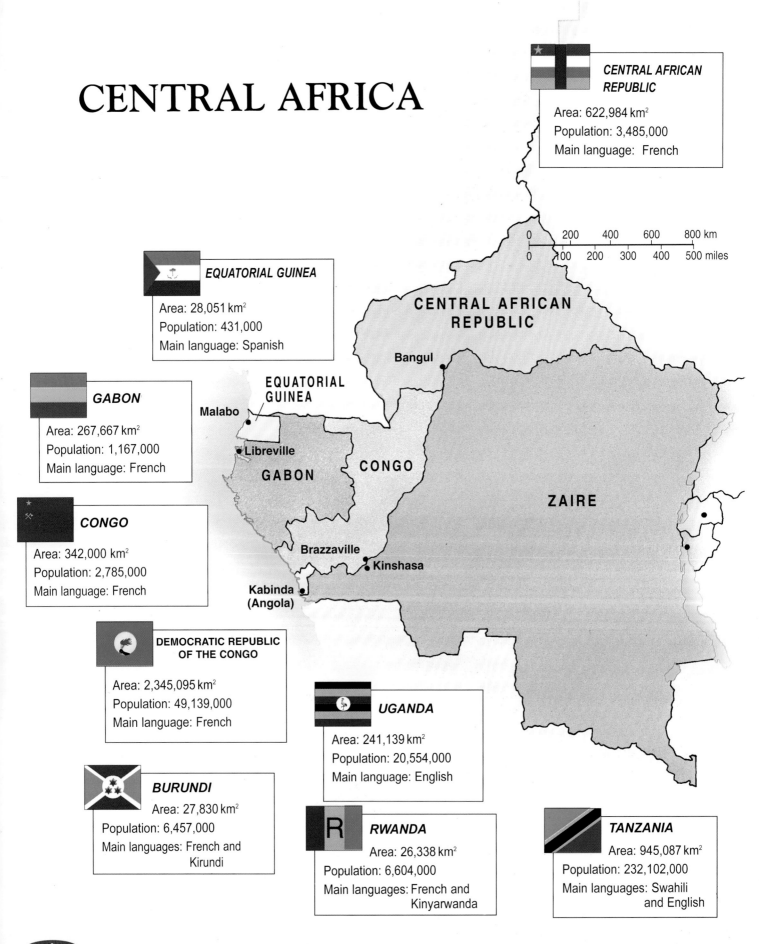

CENTRAL AFRICAN REPUBLIC
Area: 622,984 km²
Population: 3,485,000
Main language: French

200 400 600 800 km
100 200 300 400 500 miles

CENTRAL AFRICAN REPUBLIC

Bangul

EQUATORIAL GUINEA
Area: 28,051 km²
Population: 431,000
Main language: Spanish

EQUATORIAL GUINEA

Malabo

GABON
Area: 267,667 km²
Population: 1,167,000
Main language: French

Libreville

GABON

CONGO

CONGO
Area: 342,000 km²
Population: 2,785,000
Main language: French

ZAIRE

Brazzaville

Kinshasa

Kabinda (Angola)

DEMOCRATIC REPUBLIC OF THE CONGO
Area: 2,345,095 km²
Population: 49,139,000
Main language: French

UGANDA
Area: 241,139 km²
Population: 20,554,000
Main language: English

BURUNDI
Area: 27,830 km²
Population: 6,457,000
Main languages: French and Kirundi

RWANDA
Area: 26,338 km²
Population: 6,604,000
Main languages: French and Kinyarwanda

TANZANIA
Area: 945,087 km²
Population: 232,102,000
Main languages: Swahili and English

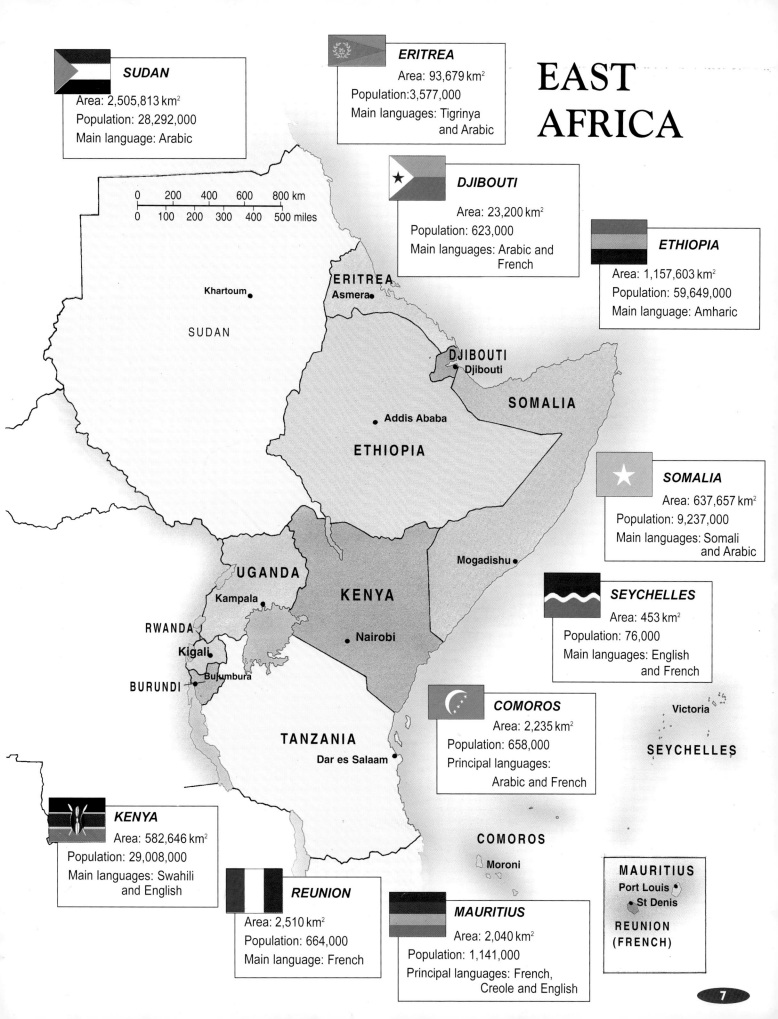

EAST AFRICA

SUDAN
Area: 2,505,813 km²
Population: 28,292,000
Main language: Arabic

ERITREA
Area: 93,679 km²
Population: 3,577,000
Main languages: Tigrinya and Arabic

DJIBOUTI
Area: 23,200 km²
Population: 623,000
Main languages: Arabic and French

ETHIOPIA
Area: 1,157,603 km²
Population: 59,649,000
Main language: Amharic

SOMALIA
Area: 637,657 km²
Population: 9,237,000
Main languages: Somali and Arabic

SEYCHELLES
Area: 453 km²
Population: 76,000
Main languages: English and French

COMOROS
Area: 2,235 km²
Population: 658,000
Principal languages: Arabic and French

KENYA
Area: 582,646 km²
Population: 29,008,000
Main languages: Swahili and English

REUNION
Area: 2,510 km²
Population: 664,000
Main language: French

MAURITIUS
Area: 2,040 km²
Population: 1,141,000
Principal languages: French, Creole and English

MAURITIUS
Port Louis
St Denis

**REUNION
(FRENCH)**

Scale:
0 200 400 600 800 km
0 100 200 300 400 500 miles

Khartoum
SUDAN
ERITREA
Asmera
DJIBOUTI
Djibouti
Addis Ababa
ETHIOPIA
SOMALIA
Mogadishu
UGANDA
Kampala
RWANDA
Kigali
BURUNDI
Bujumbura
KENYA
Nairobi
TANZANIA
Dar es Salaam
Victoria
SEYCHELLES
COMOROS
Moroni

SOUTHERN AFRICA

Luanda

ANGOLA

NAMIBIA

Walvis Bay
(S. AFRICA)

Windhoek

BOTSWANA

Gaborone ●

Mbabane ●

SWAZILAND

SOUTH
AFRICA

● **Maseru**
LESOTHO

Cape Town

ANGOLA

Area: 1,246,700 km²
Population: 12,092,000
Mainl language: Portuguese

NAMIBIA

Area: 823,144 km²
Population: 1,660,000
Main languages: English
and Afrikaans

BOTSWANA

Area: 582,000 km²
Population: 1,570,000
Main languages: Tswana
and English

SOUTH AFRICA

Area: 1,123,226 km²
Population: 39,357,000
Main languages: Afrikaans and
English

| 0 | 200 | 400 | 600 km |
| 0 | 100 | 200 | 300 | 400 miles |

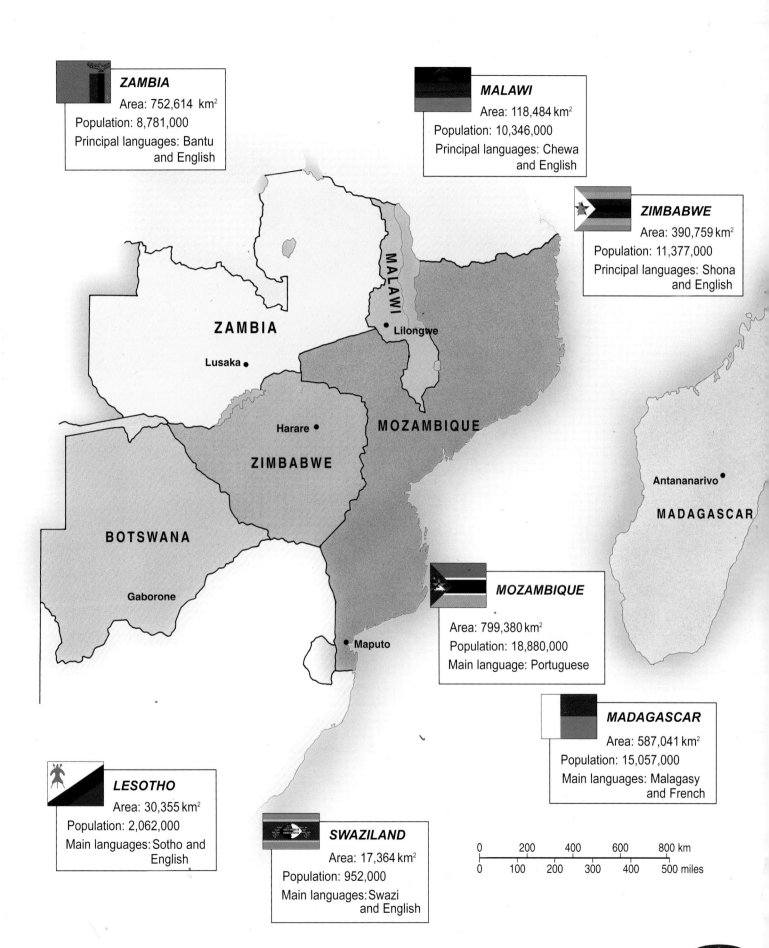

ZAMBIA
Area: 752,614 km²
Population: 8,781,000
Principal languages: Bantu and English

MALAWI
Area: 118,484 km²
Population: 10,346,000
Principal languages: Chewa and English

ZIMBABWE
Area: 390,759 km²
Population: 11,377,000
Principal languages: Shona and English

ZAMBIA

Lusaka

MALAWI

Lilongwe

MOZAMBIQUE

Harare

ZIMBABWE

BOTSWANA

Gaborone

Maputo

Antananarivo

MADAGASCAR

MOZAMBIQUE
Area: 799,380 km²
Population: 18,880,000
Main language: Portuguese

MADAGASCAR
Area: 587,041 km²
Population: 15,057,000
Main languages: Malagasy and French

LESOTHO
Area: 30,355 km²
Population: 2,062,000
Main languages: Sotho and English

SWAZILAND
Area: 17,364 km²
Population: 952,000
Main languages: Swazi and English

| 0 | 200 | 400 | 600 | 800 km |
| 0 | 100 | 200 | 300 | 400 | 500 miles |

A VAST CONTINENT

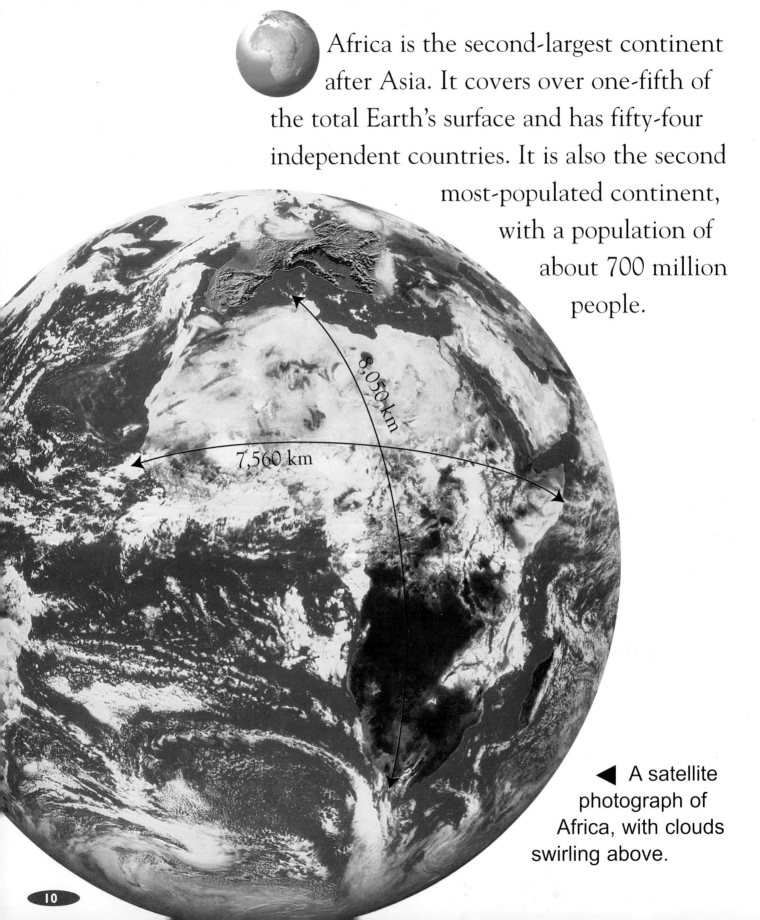

Africa is the second-largest continent after Asia. It covers over one-fifth of the total Earth's surface and has fifty-four independent countries. It is also the second most-populated continent, with a population of about 700 million people.

8,050 km

7,560 km

◄ A satellite photograph of Africa, with clouds swirling above.

◀ Thick rainforests grow near the Equator.

TROPIC OF CANCER

EQUATOR

TROPIC OF CAPRICORN

▲ The Equator and the tropics.

The Equator runs right through the middle of Africa. The tropic of Cancer runs across the north, and the tropic of Capricorn cuts across the south.

Millions of years ago, Africa was joined to South America. If you look at the coastlines of the two continents, you can see how they used to fit together. About 100 million years ago, the continents slowly started to move apart.

This globe shows the continents ▶ 50 million years ago.

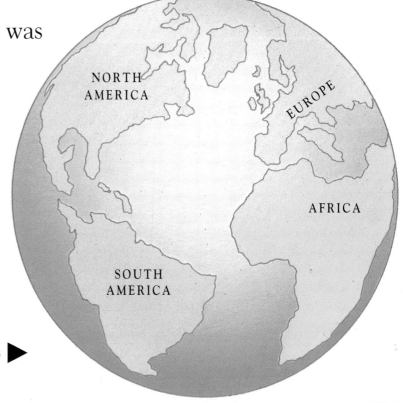

NORTH AMERICA

EUROPE

AFRICA

SOUTH AMERICA

LAND AND CLIMATE

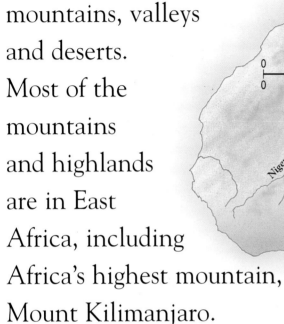
There are many different landscapes in Africa, including mountains, valleys and deserts. Most of the mountains and highlands are in East Africa, including Africa's highest mountain, Mount Kilimanjaro.

▼ This map shows Africa's rivers and deserts.

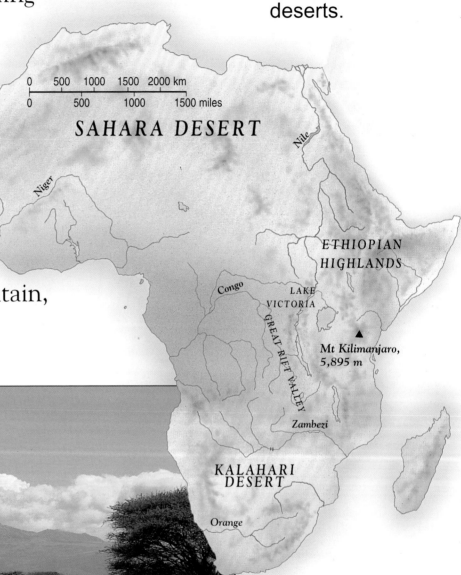

0 500 1000 1500 2000 km
0   500   1000   1500 miles

SAHARA DESERT

Nile

Niger

ETHIOPIAN
HIGHLANDS

Congo

LAKE
VICTORIA

GREAT RIFT VALLEY

Mt Kilimanjaro,
5,895 m

Zambezi

KALAHARI
DESERT

Orange

◄ Mount Kilimanjaro, in Tanzania, is 5,895 metres high.

◀ The Great Rift Valley cuts through East Africa from north to south. It contains many large lakes.

▼ The Nile is the longest river in the world. It begins in Burundi and its total length is 6,670 km.

RIVERS

Africa's major rivers include the Nile, the Congo, the Niger, the Zambezi and the Orange. Many of these rivers have huge waterfalls, such as the Victoria Falls, on the Zambezi river.

DESERTS

Africa has two large deserts: the Sahara Desert in the north and the Kalahari Desert in the south. The Sahara Desert is the largest desert in the world. People live on the edges of the deserts, but over the last thirty years the rains have been getting less. It has become much harder to grow crops and people have suffered from famine.

▼ The Sahara Desert covers a quarter of Africa's total land area. It is 5,000 km wide.

LIVING ON THE EDGE OF A DESERT

Messoud Ould Jiddou is 13 years old. He describes living on the edge of the Sahara:

"When my parents were young, there was enough rainfall in most years to feed the crops and fill the wells. Now, even during the wet season, we can't be sure of enough rainfall.

There are more people sharing the land now and my mother says she has to go much further to find firewood for cooking. There are hardly any trees left, so the land has no shelter from the sun or the wind. My father says the land is becoming poorer every year because the soil is being eroded.

We need help from aid organizations to survive. My village are getting help to plant a new forest. We will protect the new trees because we know that in the future, they will give us fruit, firewood and protection from the sun and wind."

CLIMATE AND VEGETATION

Africa's climate and vegetation depend on the distance from the Equator. The areas closest to the Equator are the wettest. This is where tropical rainforests grow. Where the rainforests are cleared, many different crops can be grown, such as bananas, cassava, yams, tea and coffee.

▼ This map shows the different types of vegetation in Africa.

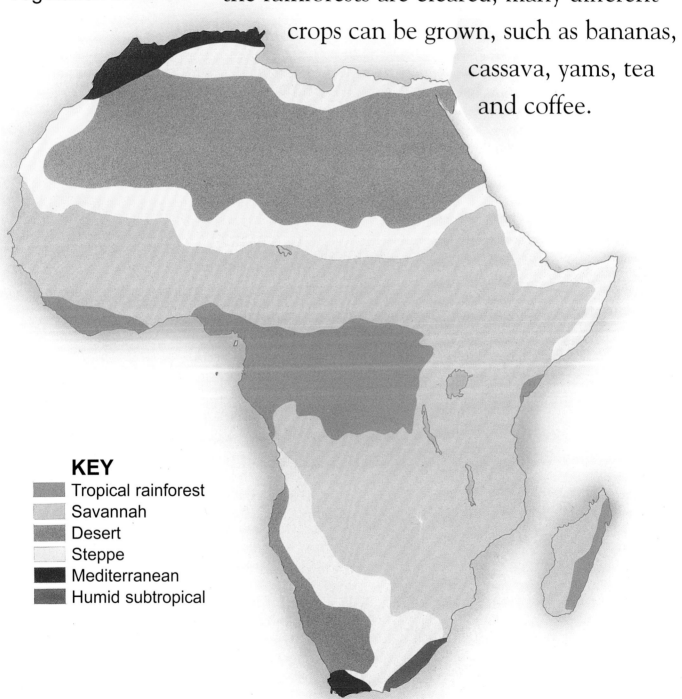

KEY

- Tropical rainforest
- Savannah
- Desert
- Steppe
- Mediterranean
- Humid subtropical

Further north and south, the climate gets drier and the vegetation turns into savannah grassland. There is a rainy season, which lasts for four to eight months. In the rainy season, cereal crops such as maize and sorghum can be grown.

▲ A tea plantation in Kenya.

◄ The Equator, the tropic of Cancer and the tropic of Capricorn.

◄ This farmer is irrigating his land using the water from the River Nile, in Egypt.

HISTORY

The first people lived in Africa almost 5 million years ago. At first they hunted and fished for food, wandering from place to place. Then, in about 4000 BC, people began to settle along the Nile, in Egypt, and learned how to make tools.

Later, powerful African kingdoms grew up in East and West Africa. They traded gold, salt and other goods with Arabia.

▼ The three most powerful African kingdoms and their trade routes.

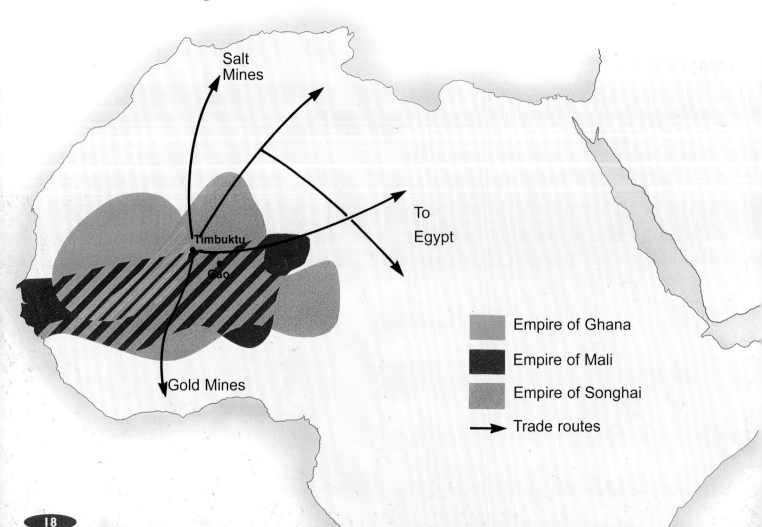

Salt Mines

To Egypt

Timbuktu

Gao

Gold Mines

Empire of Ghana

Empire of Mali

Empire of Songhai

→ Trade routes

▲ Goods were carried on camels on trade routes across the Sahara Desert.

◄ Cities on the east coast grew rich from trade in about AD 1200.

▼ Boats called dhows carried goods from Africa to Arabia.

Map labels:
500 1000 1500 km
500 1000 miles
PERSIAN GULF
ARABIA
Nile
RED SEA
Mogadishu
Malindi
Mombasa
Pemba
Zanzibar
INDIAN OCEAN
Kilwa
Zambezi
Mozambique
Sofala

COLONIAL TIMES

In the 1500s, Portuguese sea captains took over many trading cities in East Africa. Then, between 1600 and 1900, other Europeans began to explore and take over the rest of Africa. By the beginning of the 1900s, most of Africa was divided into colonies controlled by European countries, including Britain, Belgium, France, Germany, Italy and Portugal.

▼ Two British explorers, Richard Burton and John Speke, at a king's court in Central Africa.

SLAVE TRADE

Before the 1500s, traders from Arabia had shipped slaves from Africa to India, Turkey and Persia.

In the 1500s, the African slave trade grew fast as slaves were shipped to America to work on plantations there.

The slave trade caused massive suffering to Africans and created huge wealth for Europeans. It was banned in England in 1772. In America, the slave trade was banned in 1865 after the American Civil War.

THE TRADE TRIANGLE

Tobacco, cotton, sugar and rum to Europe

Brandy Firearms Iron goods Cloth

NORTH AMERICA

SOUTH AMERICA

EUROPE

AFRICA

Slaves from Africa

▼ This map shows the numbers of slaves leaving each area from 1526–1870.

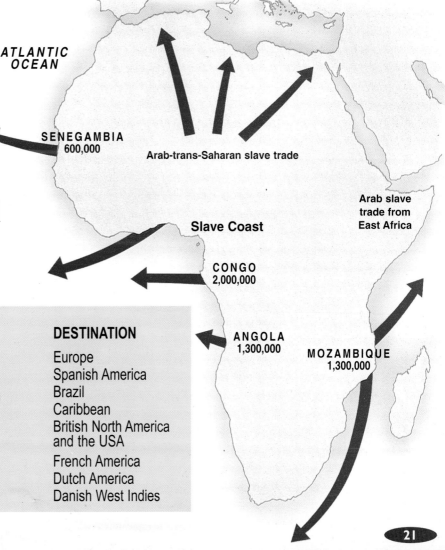

ATLANTIC OCEAN

SENEGAMBIA 600,000

Arab-trans-Saharan slave trade

Slave Coast

CONGO 2,000,000

ANGOLA 1,300,000

Arab slave trade from East Africa

MOZAMBIQUE 1,300,000

NUMBER OF SLAVES	DESTINATION
175,000	Europe
1,552,000	Spanish America
3,647,000	Brazil
1,665,000	Caribbean
399,000	British North America and the USA
1,600,000	French America
500,000	Dutch America
28,000	Danish West Indies

INDEPENDENCE

Throughout the twentieth century, most African countries became independent. But in many countries, there has been conflict and violence as new rulers have taken control.

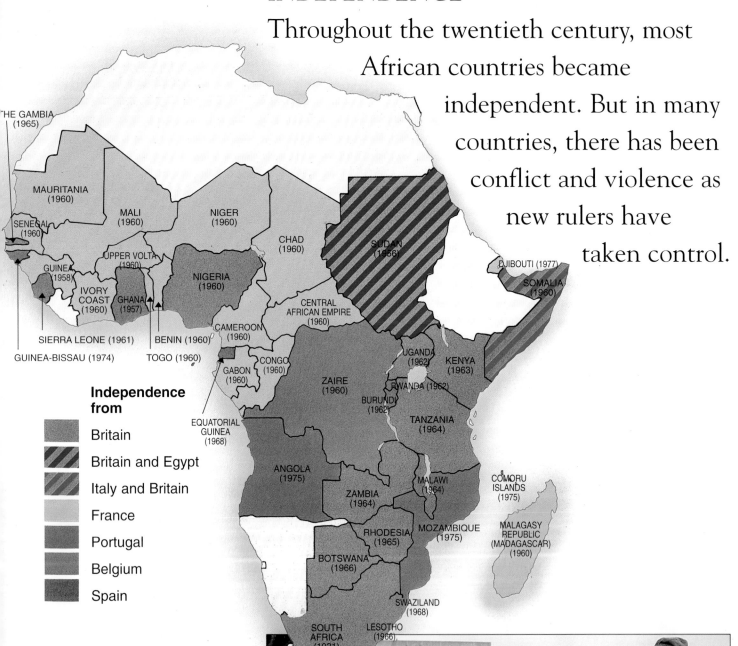

THE GAMBIA (1965)

MAURITANIA (1960)

SENEGAL (1960)

MALI (1960)

NIGER (1960)

CHAD (1960)

SUDAN (1956)

DJIBOUTI (1977)

SOMALIA (1960)

GUINEA (1958)

UPPER VOLTA (1960)

IVORY COAST (1960)

GHANA (1957)

NIGERIA (1960)

CENTRAL AFRICAN EMPIRE (1960)

SIERRA LEONE (1961)

BENIN (1960)

CAMEROON (1960)

GUINEA-BISSAU (1974)

TOGO (1960)

GABON (1960)

CONGO (1960)

UGANDA (1962)

KENYA (1963)

ZAIRE (1960)

RWANDA (1962)

BURUNDI (1962)

TANZANIA (1964)

EQUATORIAL GUINEA (1968)

Independence from

- Britain
- Britain and Egypt
- Italy and Britain
- France
- Portugal
- Belgium
- Spain

ANGOLA (1975)

ZAMBIA (1964)

MALAWI (1964)

COMORU ISLANDS (1975)

RHODESIA (1965)

MOZAMBIQUE (1975)

MALAGASY REPUBLIC (MADAGASCAR) (1960)

BOTSWANA (1966)

SWAZILAND (1968)

SOUTH AFRICA (1931)

LESOTHO (1966)

In Rwanda, in ▶ 1994, bitter fighting broke out between rival ethnic groups, the Tutsi and the Hutu.

◀ People protesting against the system of apartheid in South Africa, in 1994. Apartheid unfairly separated whites from blacks in South Africa, and kept the white government in power.

DEMOCRACY

The biggest struggle for African countries has been to gain democratic rule, where the government is chosen by the majority of the population. In some countries, differences in racial and tribal groups caused conflict, such as in Rwanda and South Africa. In others, such as in Nigeria, African rulers ignored democratic elections and seized power.

◀ In 1994, apartheid was stopped. Nelson Mandela became South Africa's first black president, after the country's first democratic elections.

RESOURCES

Only one-fifth of Africa's land is suitable for farming, and much of that soil is too poor to grow crops. So Africa relies heavily on food aid to feed its growing population.

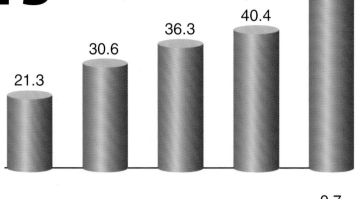

FOOD PRODUCTION
(millions of tonnes)

21.3 30.6 36.3 40.4 55.8

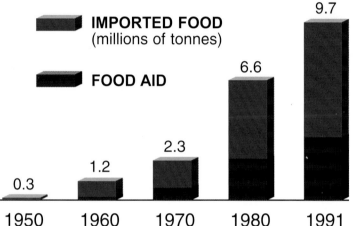

IMPORTED FOOD
(millions of tonnes)

FOOD AID

9.7   6.6   2.3   1.2   0.3

| 1950 | 1960 | 1970 | 1980 | 1991 |

▲ Africa's food production is increasing, but its food imports and aid from abroad are increasing even faster.

▲ Cocoa beans are a major export crop for Africa.

In 1992, food ▶ aid to Africa increased to over 6 million tonnes when a famine struck Ethiopia.

FOOD AID TO AFRICA, 1989–1998

	Millions of tonnes
1989	2.9
1990	3.0
1991	3.8
1992	6.0
1993	5.0
1994	4.0
1995	3.2
1996	2.8
1997	2.5
1998	2.9

◀ Machines are used on large farms and plantations, like this one in Tanzania.

TECHNOLOGY AND IRRIGATION

Most African farmers cannot afford to use machinery, irrigation or fertilizers, which would help them grow more food crops. This is because most farmers are small, 'subsistence' farmers, who do not produce enough food to sell for cash.

Only a few farmers can afford to use machinery and fertilizers. They own large estates or plantations, which were started in colonial times.

▼ This graph shows that women are very important farm workers in Africa.

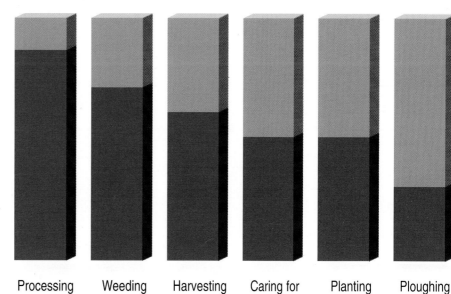

Men
Women

Processing and storing crops

Weeding

Harvesting

Caring for livestock

Planting

Ploughing

MINING

Africa has vast deposits of minerals for mining, but little manufacturing industry. So most of its minerals are exported to other countries, and expensive manufactured goods are imported from abroad. This means that Africa is earning less than it is selling, and is becoming poorer. Many African countries are in debt.

▲ This car assembly factory was set up recently in Nigeria. It provides work for local people.

AFRICAN MINERALS

Mineral	% of World Reserves
Chrome	99%
Platinum	85%
Tantalite	68%
Cobalt	68%
Gold	54%

Other important minerals

Diamonds	Bauxite
Oil	

▼ A bauxite mine in Guinea.

COPPER MINING IN ZAMBIA

Many African countries rely on one mineral for their income. When the price of the mineral drops, the whole country suffers. Tambala Tschombe remembers this happening in Zambia:

"During the 1960s and early 1970s, there were very good prices for copper on the international market. But from 1975–1986, the prices fell. This was a disaster – many workers lost their jobs. It was also very difficult for our country, as we could buy much less from other countries with the money we earned from selling copper. Although the price of copper has improved since the 1980s, it will be a long time before our country really benefits from its natural resources."

Tourism is a growing industry in Africa. It relies on Africa's landscapes, wildlife and cultures.

▲ A copper mine in Zaire.

TOURIST	ATTRACTIONS
Serengeti Plain	Moroccan bazaars
Egyptian pyramids	Victoria Falls
Mt Kilimanjaro	The Gambia
Safari in Kruger National Park	Boat trip down the Nile River

Tourists on safari in ▶ Tanzania.

PEOPLE AND RELIGIONS

The two biggest religious groups in Africa are Christianity and Islam. There are also other religions, including a number of traditional African religions. Many people mix elements of a traditional African religion with Christianity or Islam.

ISLAM

Islam came to Africa from Arabia in the seventh century. Over the last 100 years, it has been growing rapidly. Today most Muslims live in North and East Africa.

▼ Muslims praying in a Cairo mosque.

CHRISTIANITY

Christianity came to Africa in the first century AD. It grew with the Portuguese and other Europeans from the fifteenth century. From the eighteenth century, missionaries and colonists spread Christianity further.

▲ Archbishop Desmond Tutu in South Africa.

Since the 1950s, many new Christian churches have started and grown in Africa, such as the Jehovah's Witnesses.

TRADITIONAL RELIGIONS

▼ This shrine is for a traditional religion's goddess, in Nigeria.

Traditional African religions help explain the forces of nature, such as a bad harvest. There are a number of gods, including ancestors, who look after the living, and leaders such as rainmakers who have special powers.

POPULATION

Over the last 35 years, millions of Africans have moved to the cities from the countryside, in search of better jobs, money, schools and quality of life. Many Africans live in the nearest city, and send money home to their family in the countryside.

Not all cities have enough houses, water or other services to cope with such numbers, so many people now live in shanty towns on the city outskirts.

Civil wars, like the one in Rwanda in 1994, have forced millions of Africans out of their home countries.

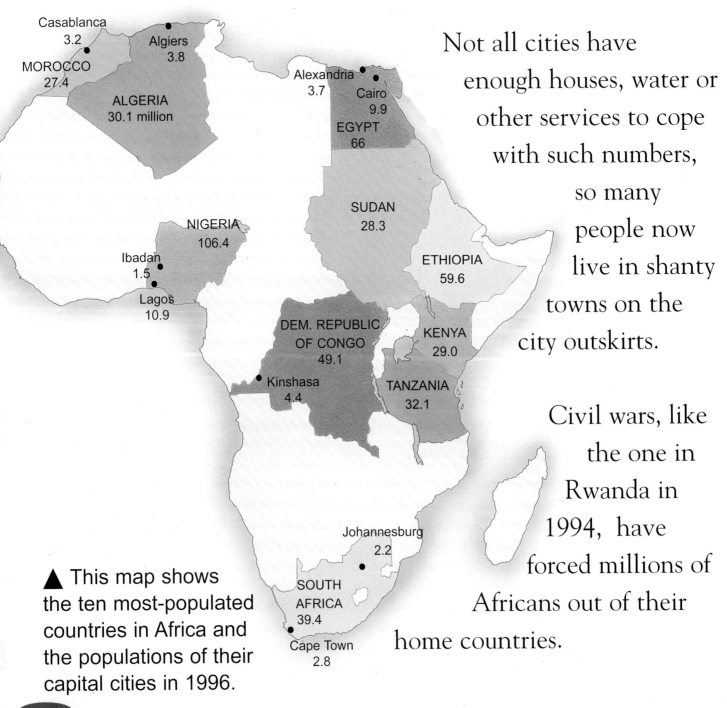

Casablanca
3.2
MOROCCO
27.4
Algiers
3.8
ALGERIA
30.1 million
Alexandria
3.7
Cairo
9.9
EGYPT
66
SUDAN
28.3
NIGERIA
106.4
Ibadan
1.5
Lagos
10.9
ETHIOPIA
59.6
DEM. REPUBLIC
OF CONGO
49.1
Kinshasa
4.4
KENYA
29.0
TANZANIA
32.1
Johannesburg
2.2
SOUTH
AFRICA
39.4
Cape Town
2.8

▲ This map shows the ten most-populated countries in Africa and the populations of their capital cities in 1996.

▲ Refugees from Rwanda, in 1994, staying in neighbouring Zaire.

CITIES AND POPULATION

- In 1998, the total population of Africa was 748.9 million. By 2025, it is predicted to grow to 1.3 billion.

- Nigeria is the most populated country in Africa. In 1998 it was the tenth most-populated country in the world.

- Lagos is Africa's most populated city. In 1996, it was the world's twelfth most populated city. By 2015, it is estimated it will rise to third place.

- Between 1975 and 1995, the city of Lagos more than doubled it population, growing by 212%. Lusaka, in Zambia, grew by 243% and Nairobi in Kenya grew by 167%.

- The African countries with the highest levels of population density are Rwanda (251), Burundi (232) and Nigeria (115).

- In 1996, Africa had two of the world's twenty largest cities: Lagos and Cairo.

▼ A traditional village compound.

TOO MANY PEOPLE?

In 1998, Africa had a population of over 749 million and by the year 2025, it is predicted to reach 1.3 billion. The population is growing at a rate of 2.4 per cent a year, which is faster than any other continent. Some people think Africa has too many people. Others disagree. What do you think?

VIEWPOINT 1:
"Africa has too many people"

"Africa's population is predicted to almost triple by the year 2050. Most African countries do not have the resources to cope with this population explosion.

Health and education services will be overstretched, so standards will drop. Farmers will not be able to grow enough food, so people will starve, and there will be environmental damage from too many people trying to make a living from the land.

People must have smaller families. The only way to improve people's quality of life is to reduce Africa's population."

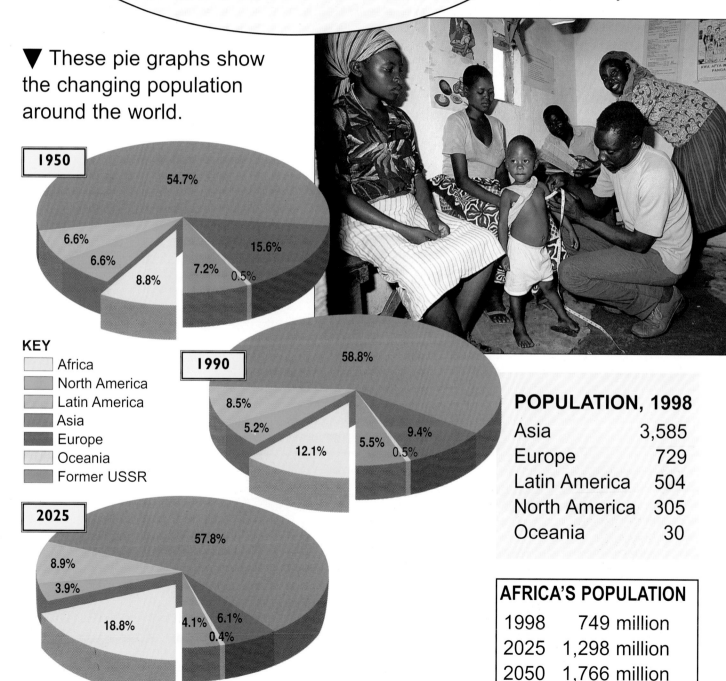

VIEWPOINT 2:
"Africa does not have too many people"

"Africa can produce enough food for its people, but governments need to help small farmers, not just the wealthy ones. If conditions in the countryside are improved and jobs are created, people will not need to move to the cities."

▼ Africa needs more health clinics like this one in the countryside.

▼ These pie graphs show the changing population around the world.

1950

54.7%

6.6%

6.6%

8.8%

7.2%

0.5%

15.6%

KEY
- Africa
- North America
- Latin America
- Asia
- Europe
- Oceania
- Former USSR

1990

58.8%

8.5%

5.2%

12.1%

5.5%

0.5%

9.4%

2025

57.8%

8.9%

3.9%

18.8%

4.1%

0.4%

6.1%

POPULATION, 1998

Asia	3,585
Europe	729
Latin America	504
North America	305
Oceania	30

AFRICA'S POPULATION

1998	749 million
2025	1,298 million
2050	1,766 million

DEVELOPMENT

Development is a word used to describe how poor countries get richer and quality of life improves. But how can you measure quality of life? There are a number of different ways, including life expectancy, education levels and infant mortality rates.

▼ The numbers of children going to school in Africa are increasing.

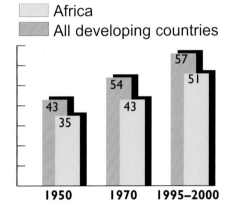

	1950	1970	1995–2000
All developing countries	43	54	57
Africa	35	43	51

▲ Life expectancy at birth (years)

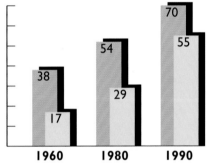

	1960	1980	1990
All developing countries	38	54	70
Africa	17	29	55

▲ Adult literacy rate (% of population)

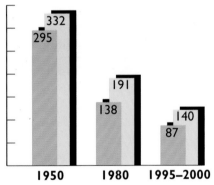

	1950	1980	1995–2000
All developing countries	332	191	140
Africa	295	138	87

Under 5-infant mortality rate (per 1000 births)

AFRICA'S DEVELOPMENT

Africa has developed slower than other continents over the past 100 years, but there has been real progress in life expectancy, health, education, access to clean water, sanitation and nutrition. There are also big differences between countries.

• Between 1960–95: life expectancy rose from 41 to 51 years, and the number of children dying before they reached 5 years old (under-5 infant mortality rate) dropped from 360 to 140.

• In African cities, over 80 per cent of children now have access to safe drinking water.

• In 1998, in Sierra Leone, the under-5 infant mortality rate was 263 per 1000 births; in Tunisia it was 37 per 1000 births.

• In 1998, in Uganda, life expectancy was 40 years; in the same year in Algeria, life expectancy was 69 years.

LITERACY IN AFRICA

Adults over 15 years old who can read and write

Women	35%
Men	60%

Many African countries have ▶ now immunized their children against major diseases.

THREE DIFFERENT COUNTRIES

Mozambique, Botswana and Algeria are three examples of very different countries. You can compare their levels of development in the fact boxes below.

Mozambique

Mozambique is one of the world's poorest countries. A civil war between 1976 and 1992 made food production drop. Its infant mortality rate is the tenth-worst in the world.

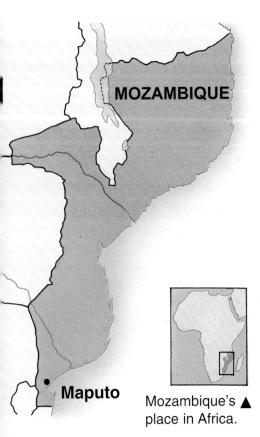

MOZAMBIQUE

Literacy rate: 38%
Life expectancy: 44 yrs
Under 5-infant mortality
rate (per 1000 births): 206

MOZAMBIQUE

Maputo

Mozambique's ▲ place in Africa.

▼ Mozambique relies on food aid from abroad.

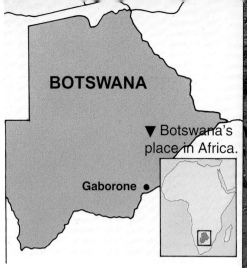

BOTSWANA

Gaborone •

▼ Botswana's place in Africa.

A successful small ▶ farm in Botswana.

BOTSWANA

Literacy rate: 73%
Life expectancy: 47 yrs
Under 5-infant mortality rate (per 1000 births): 48

Botswana

Botswana has developed well since 1960. Its income per person is one of the highest in Africa, literacy rates have increased and infant mortality rates have fallen.

ALGERIA

Literacy rate: 58%
Life expectancy: 69 yrs
Under 5-infant mortality rate (per 1000 births): 40

Algeria

Algeria is one of Africa's richest countries, but it relies heavily on its oil industries, so when oil prices fall, living standards fall too.

Algeria relies on its oil and gas industries. ▶

Algiers •

ALGERIA

◀ Algeria's place in Africa.

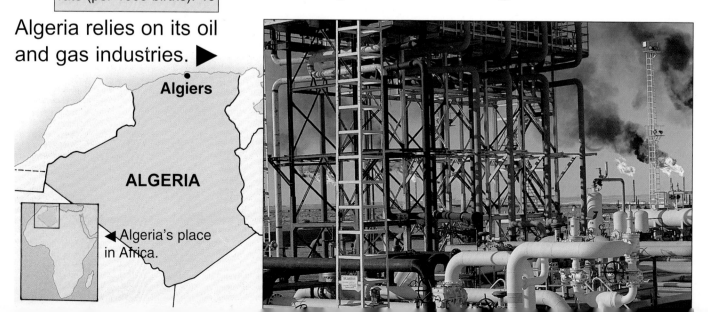

FAMINE IN ETHIOPIA

In 1984 over a million people died in a famine in Ethiopia. Drought was partly to blame for the disaster, but the famine was caused by more than just drought.

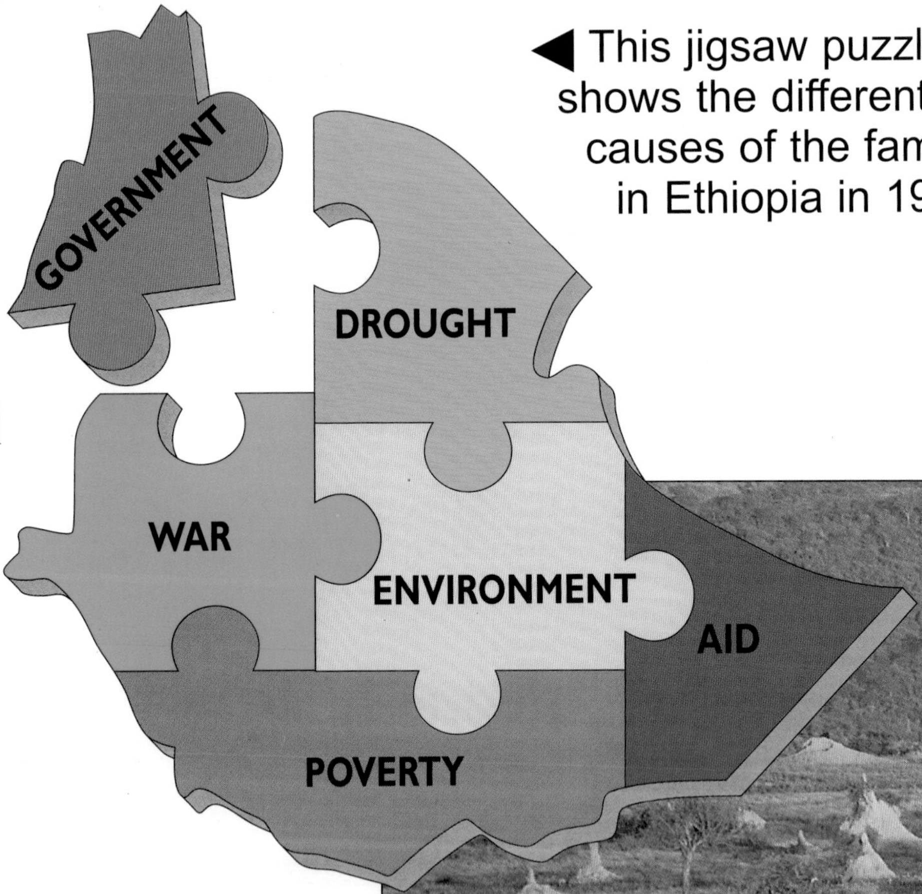

Government

From 1930–74, Emperor Haile Selassie ruled Ethiopia and did little to help farmers. The country grew poorer.

War

From 1961–91, civil war drained money that could have been spent on developing industry.

Poverty

There is little industry in Ethiopia, so most people rely on farming for a living.

GOVERNMENT

DROUGHT

WAR

ENVIRONMENT

AID

POVERTY

◀ This jigsaw puzzle shows the different causes of the famine in Ethiopia in 1984.

Drought

There were several droughts throughout the 1970s and early 1980s. In 1983, there was hardly any rain.

▲ A relief centre for famine victims.

Environment

Soil erosion caused by deforestation made crop farming even harder.

▼ A refugee camp.

Aid

Not enough aid arrived from abroad in the early 1980s. The food that did arrive had trouble getting to people.

ETHIOPIA FACTS

Literacy rate: 33%

Life expectancy: 43 yrs

Under 5-infant mortality rate (per 1000 births): 173

ENVIRONMENT

Deforestation and soil erosion are big problems in Africa.

DEFORESTATION

Deforestation is caused by people using wood for fuel, clearing forested areas to create new farmland and by logging industries. Africa's growing population has put a lot of pressure on the land, and many trees have been lost. When trees are cut down, there are no roots to hold the soil in place so deforestation also causes soil erosion.

▲ This map shows areas threatened by deforestation.

◄ In many parts of Africa, cattle overgraze the land and strip away too much grass. The land cannot recover.

SOIL EROSION

Soil erosion in Africa is also caused by overploughing, overgrazing and poor irrigation, all of which are caused by poverty and a growing population. Soil is essential for growing food crops to feed a country's population.

African farmers need help to build irrigation schemes and use modern farming methods.

▲ Many African elephants have been killed for their ivory, yet countries depend on their wildlife for their tourist industry.

HOW THE ENVIRONMENT AFFECTS PEOPLE

Lack of rainfall	Drought, poor harvests, hunger
Storms	Soil erosion and nutrition loss, water loss
Soil with low clay content	Poor soil because it is unable to hold water and nutrients.
Few places with shallow water	Increased work carrying water to homes and fields.

AFRICA AND THE WORLD

Africa's natural resources made it a powerful world trader in the past. But the prices of goods that Africa exports have dropped, while the prices of imports have risen. African leaders are trying to raise the price of their exported goods so the rest of the world pays more. This will help them reduce their national debts.

ART, MUSIC AND LITERATURE

African art and music can be seen all over the world today, including masks, jewellery, design, sculpture and the rhythms of world music and dance.

▲ Douglas Wakihuru is one of many world-class Kenyan athletes.

WANGARI MAATHAI

In 1989, Professor Wangari Maathai was made 'Woman of the World' for setting up the Green Belt movement in Kenya, which helps communities plant trees.

WOLE SOYINKA (born 1934)

Nigerian writer Wole Soyinka was the first African to be awarded the Nobel prize for literature.

BOUTROS BOUTROS-GHALI (born 1992)

Egyptian-born Boutros Boutros-Ghali was Secretary-General of the United Nations from 1992–96.

▲ Wole Soyinka writes poetry, novels and plays.

◀ Boutros-Ghali was the first African and the first Arab to be made Secretary-General of the United Nations. He was replaced by Ghana-born Kofi Annan in 1997.

TIMELINE

BC

4000 Early settlements along the banks of the Nile.

3500 Kingdom of the Pharaohs established on the Nile.

2500 Cultures using metals appear along the coast of North Africa.

1000 Early cultivation in both East and West Africa. Bantu-speaking Africans spread outwards from North Africa.

671 Assyrian conquest of Egypt.

520 Darius I completes the canal connecting the Nile with the Red Sea.

334 Alexander the Great conquers Egypt.

30 Death of Antony and Cleopatra. Egypt becomes a Roman province.

AD

44 Morocco annexed by Rome.

641 Arabs conquer Egypt and begin conquest of North Africa.

700–800 Arabs conquer North Africa and convert the local people to Islam. Arab traders establish trading towns on the east coast.

1400s European explorers seeking a sea route to Asia discover much of the African coast and trade with African tribes, bringing gold and ivory to Europe.

1498 Portuguese explorer, Vasco da Gama, rounds the Cape of Good Hope and sails on to India. Portuguese introduce Christianity to large parts of Africa.

1500s Other European powers become involved in Africa and begin to take over part of the Portuguese trade.

1546 Destruction of the Mali empire by Songhay.

1571 Portuguese create colony in Angola.

1578 Moroccans destroy Portuguese power in northwest Africa.

1652 Foundation of Cape Colony by Dutch.

1659 French found trading station on Senegal coast.

1662 Battle of Ambuila: destruction of Kongo kingdom by Portuguese.

1700 Rise of Asante power (Gold coast).

1798 Napolean attacks Egypt.

1800–1914 Africa divided between the French, Belgians, Portuguese, British, Germans and Italians.

1807 Slave trade abolished within the British Empire.

1811 Mohammed Ali takes control in Egypt.

1822 Liberia founded as colony for freed slaves.

1830 French begin conquest of Algeria.

1835 'Great Trek' of Boer colonists from Cape, leading to foundation of Republic of Natal (1839), Orange Free State (1848) Transvaal (1849).

1840s Livingstone's explorations begin.

1869 Suez Canal opens.

1881 French occupy Tunisia.

1882	Revolt in Egypt leading to British occupation.
1884	Germany acquires southwest Africa.
1886	Germany and Britain partition East Africa. Gold is discovered in Transvaal, and Johannesburg is founded.
1889	British South Africa Company formed by Cecil Rhodes, begins colonization of Rhodesia (1890).
1896	Italians defeated by Ethiopians.
1898	Fashoda crisis between Britain and France.
1899	Boer War begins.
1900–1960	African nationalism and desire for independence grows with opposition to colonial rule.
1908	Belgian state takes over Congo from King Leopold of Belgium.
1910	Foundation of Union of South Africa.
1912	Italy conquers Libya.
1914–15	French and British conquer German colonies except German East Africa.
1919	Nationalist revolt in Egypt against the British.
1930-1975	Forty-one African states become independent.
1935	Italy invades Ethiopia.
1936	Anglo-Egyptian alliance.
1940	Italians expelled from Somalia, Eritrea and Ethiopia.
1942	Germans advance into Egypt. Battle of El-Alamein: German retreat and defeat. Anglo-American landings in Morocco and Algeria.
1949	Apartheid introduced in South Africa.

1952	Beginning of Mau Mau rebellion in Kenya. Military revolt in Egypt.
1956	Beginning of decolonization in sub-Saharan Africa: Gold Coast becomes independent.
1960	'Africa's year'. Many states become independent.
1961	South Africa becomes an independent republic.
1962	Algeria becomes independent.
1965	Rhodesia declares independence.
1967	Civil war in Nigeria.
1975	Portugal grants independence to Mozambique and Angola.
1980	Black majority rule in Zimbabwe (Rhodesia).
1984	Famine in Sahel and Ethiopia.
1985	Civil unrest in South Africa.
1986	US bomb Libya for terrorist activities.
1990	Namibia becomes independent. The South African government recognizes the ANC, frees Nelson Mandela and, in 1991, starts to dismantle apartheid.
1992	US forces intervene to end Somalia's famine and civil war.
1994	President Mandela becomes president of South Africa in the first democratic elections.
1998	Civil war breaks out in the Democratic Republic of Congo
1999	Nigeria successfully elects its first civilian government after fifteen years of military rule.
2000	President Nelson Mandela steps down as president of South Africa.

GLOSSARY

Aid organisations Groups that organise the supply of food and other materials to help poor countries.

Apartheid A policy of separating white and black South Africans, which was dismantled in 1991.

Civil wars Wars within a country, usually over struggle for power.

Colony A country or area that is controlled by a foreign power.

Deforestation Cutting down large areas of forest.

Democracy A system of rule where leaders are chosen, or elected by the people.

Export Sold abroad.

Fertilizers Substances added to the soil to make it better for growing crops.

Gross National Product (GNP) The total money a country earns inside its borders, plus the money it makes from exports.

Import Buy from another country.

Immunized Protected from disease by an injection.

Independence When a colony becomes free from foreign rule.

Infant mortality Child death.

Irrigating Watering land in order to grow crops.

Literacy The ability to read and write.

Plantations Estates or large areas of farmland where crops are grown for sale.

Raw materials Materials in their natural state, such as coal or iron ore.

Resources Natural materials from a country, for example coal, iron ore, timber and fish.

Savannah A fairly dry area of usually level land covered with low vegetation and occasional small patches of woodland.

Soil erosion The wearing away of the soil by wind or rain.

Standards of living The level of wealth and services available to people for living, for example education, healthcare and consumer goods.

Shanty towns Poor, overcrowded housing.

FINDING OUT MORE

OTHER BOOKS TO READ

Ancient Egypt (History Beneath your Feet series)(Hodder Wayland, 1999)

Crisis in Central Africa (New Perspectives series)(Hodder Wayland, 1999)

East Africa (World Fact Files series)(Hodder Wayland, 1997)

Egypt (Country Fact Files series)(Hodder Wayland, 1996)

A Flavour of Kenya by Wambui Kairi (Hodder Wayland, 1999)

Kenya (Country Insights series) by Wambui Kairi (Wayland, 1997)

Life Stories: Nelson Mandela (Hodder Wayland, 1993)

Philips Geographical Digest 2000 (Heinemann Educational, 2000)

Southern Africa (World Fact Files series)(Hodder Wayland, 1997)

Stories from Africa (Hodder Wayland, 2000)

Traditions from Africa (Cultural Journeys series) (Hodder Wayland, 1998)

Wayland Atlas of Threatened Cultures (Hodder Wayland, 2000)

West Africa (World Fact Files series)(Hodder Wayland, 1997)

ADDRESSES AND WEBSITES

ActionAid, Hamlyn House, Archway, London N19 5PG.
Tel 0207 282 4101   Website: www.actionaid.org

Africa.com Website: www.africa.com

Oxfam: 274 Banbury Road, Oxford OX2 7DZ.
Tel: 01865 56777   Website: www.oxfam.org.uk

Development Education Association, 3rd Floor, Cowper Street,
London EC2A 4AP

MBendi: Information for Africa Website: http://mbendi.co

United Nations Development Programme Website: www.undp.org

Unicef: 55-6 Lincoln's Inn Fields, London WC2A 3NB.
Tel: 0207 405 5592   Website: www.unicef.org

INDEX

Page numbers in **bold** show pictures as well as text.